IT'S A DIGITAL WORLD!

Helpful Hackers

Heather C. Hudak

Checkerboard
Library

An Imprint of Abdo Publishing
abdopublishing.com

ABDOPUBLISHING.COM

Published by Abdo Publishing, a division of ABDO, PO Box 398166, Minneapolis, Minnesota 55439. Copyright © 2019 by Abdo Consulting Group, Inc. International copyrights reserved in all countries. No part of this book may be reproduced in any form without written permission from the publisher. Checkerboard Library™ is a trademark and logo of Abdo Publishing.

Printed in the United States of America, North Mankato, Minnesota
052018
092018

Design: Kelly Doudna, Mighty Media, Inc.
Production: Mighty Media, Inc.
Editor: Liz Salzmann
Cover Photographs: iStockphoto (left), Shutterstock (right)
Interior Photographs: Alamy, p. 9; AP Images, pp. 10, 17, 18, 21, 26, 28; Courtesy MIT Museum, p. 15; Daniel Ge/Flickr, p. 27; iStockphoto, p. 7; Jeff Keyzer/Flickr, pp. 25, 29; New America/Flickr, p. 22; Shutterstock, pp. 4, 13

Library of Congress Control Number: 2017961592

Publisher's Cataloging-in-Publication Data
Name: Hudak, Heather C., author.
Title: Helpful Hackers / by Heather C. Hudak.
Description: Minneapolis, Minnesota : Abdo Publishing, 2019. | Series: It's a digital world! | Includes online resources and index.
Identifiers: ISBN 9781532115349 (lib.bdg.) | ISBN 9781532156069 (ebook)
Subjects: LCSH: Hackers--Juvenile literature. | Ethical hacking (Computer security)--Juvenile literature. | Debugging in computer science--Juvenile literature. | Occupations--Careers--Jobs--Juvenile literature.
Classification: DDC 005.8092--dc23

CONTENTS

STRETCHING THE BOUNDARIES OF TECHNOLOGY

Have you ever planned a surprise party that you needed to keep secret? Did you save information about it on a computer? Maybe you used a password to keep other people from being able to read it. What if someone was able to get into your computer and read about the party? They could change the information or they could even remove it.

Hackers find weaknesses in computer systems and **software**. Most hackers try to fix problems as they find them. They have jobs in **cybersecurity** or software testing. But some hackers use their skills to harm others. They break into computer systems to steal or destroy information.

Hackers stretch the boundaries of **technology** to find new ways to use it. Hackers can visualize how to do things differently. Then they find **innovative** ways to make their visions come true.

CHAPTER 1

HOW TO BECOME A HACKER

Hackers' jobs are to invent new ways to solve problems and improve processes. Hackers have expert knowledge of computer systems and **software** and enjoy figuring out how they work. Many hackers like taking things apart and putting them back together.

Hackers look for new ways to use existing systems and software. When computer programs don't do what hackers need them to do, hackers find ways to get the job done. They may even write new computer **code**. Hackers are also good at creating new computer programs.

A college or university degree is not required to be a hacker. Hackers just need to know a lot about computers and software. Still, many hackers have degrees in computer science, information **technology** (IT), or **network** security.

Some organizations offer special **certifications** for hackers. Such certifications show that hackers have the skills

Students at the University of Illinois can apply for the Illinois Cyber Security Scholars Program. Graduates of the program have gone on to work for government agencies such as Homeland Security and the Central Intelligence Agency.

and knowledge they need to do their jobs well. Having a **certification** also shows that a hacker is trustworthy.

Some hackers work as part of a team. The whole team works together to find solutions to problems. Other hackers work alone. They work for companies on a project-by-project basis.

CHAPTER 2

BLACK HATS VS. WHITE HATS

When hackers are mentioned in the news, the story is usually about unethical hackers who have done something wrong. Unethical hackers are also called black hat hackers. This is because in old Western movies, the bad guys almost always wore black hats.

Black hat hackers break into computer systems and **software** for the purpose of harming others. They steal data and damage systems. They might steal money, invade people's privacy, or destroy documents.

Because of news coverage of hacking crimes, many people think that's all hackers do. However, most hackers are ethical. They want to make computers more secure. Ethical hackers are called white hat hackers because the good guys in Westerns usually wore white hats.

White hat hackers help protect companies from black hat hackers. Companies hire white hat hackers to break into systems

The Lone Ranger is a hero in many Western television shows and movies. He is known for wearing a white hat.

and programs to find weaknesses. Then the hackers determine how to make the systems stronger. This is called penetration testing. Hackers also help other people in their workplaces understand possible threats. They teach others how to prevent **cybercriminals** from harming their systems and **software**.

White hat hackers keep an eye on the data that flows in and out of their companies' servers each day. They watch for security threats and weaknesses where black hat hackers could break into the systems. They make sure the company's connection to the internet is as secure as possible.

Cybersecurity isn't the only way hackers use their skills. Some hackers test new games, apps, and software programs before they are released. These hackers look for any problems and make sure these products work properly. When hackers

American Kevin Mitnick was the first hacker to be on the FBI's Most Wanted list. In the 1990s, he spent several years in jail for hacking. Later, he became a white hat hacker and started a cybersecurity consulting business.

find problems, they may work with the original programmers to fix them. Or they might fix the problems themselves.

White hat and black hat hackers use the same programs and methods. There are many programs they can use. Some programs help hackers enter private **networks** or computer systems. White hat hackers are allowed to enter these systems. Black hat hackers are not.

Cain & Abel and Aircrack-ng are programs that help hackers find peoples' passwords. Other programs help hackers test **software** and security. Hackers use software programs Wireshark and Nmap to see who is connecting to a computer network and perform security tests. They use programs such as Omnipeek to watch and report on wireless traffic.

OPEN SOURCE CODE

Many hackers share the programs they use so they can learn from one another. They make their computer source **code available** to others to use for free. Source code is a series of instructions, comments, and functions that tells a computer what to do. It is part of any software program. Source code that is shared freely is called open source code.

CHAPTER 3
STOPPING SECURITY THREATS

Hackers can be helpful to all types of companies, big or small. Any companies that use computer **networks** or the internet are at risk for security threats. Companies hire white hat hackers to tell them what they need to do to protect themselves.

Large organizations, such as governments, hospitals, banks, and universities have thousands of people connecting to their systems. Each of these people has a computer and other devices that contain important information. This information could include top-secret military activities, ground-breaking research, or credit card details. In the wrong hands, this information could be used to hurt people or steal from them. White hat hackers help find ways to protect these devices from security threats.

In addition to trying to hack into systems, black hat hackers often use **scams**. They contact people through email or websites and pretend to be trustworthy. They might say they are from a government agency or a reputable company such as Google.

Then they ask for personal or sensitive information, such as credit card or Social Security numbers. The hackers could use this information to buy expensive products or steal the person's identity. White hat hackers show people how to recognize these **scams** and avoid giving information to the wrong people.

Between 2005 and 2007, a group of hackers stole 45.6 million credit card numbers from TJX Companies. TJX owns several retail brands, including T.J. Maxx. The hacker group's leader, Albert Gonzalez, was sentenced to 20 years in prison.

CHAPTER 4

HACKER HISTORY

The word hack hasn't always been associated with computers. The word has been part of the English language for hundreds of years and has many different meanings. One meaning is "to cut or chop with uneven or unskillful blows."

During the 1960s, *hack* started being associated with computer programming. Students at Massachusetts Institute of **Technology** (MIT) began using computer programming in new and creative ways. *Hacking* was used to describe these new methods.

At the time, modern computers were just starting to be developed. So, these were the types of systems people began to hack. This was how scientists and engineers came up with new and better ways to use computers.

During the mid-1900s, hackers were people who had big ideas about what they could do with computers. They stretched the capabilities of computer systems. They began working on

An early group to use the term *hack* was the Tech Model Railroad Club at MIT. Club members used *hack* to refer to inventing new ways to set up electrical circuits for model trains.

ways to connect computers to one another so they could share information. This was the beginning of computer **networks**.

Hackers were considered the best at what they did by their peers in computer science. These **innovators** pushed the boundaries of **technology** and what it could do. Their ideas and advancements led to the development of the internet, smartphones, and other technologies. Hackers helped change the world.

CHAPTER 5
INTENT TO HARM

Computers started becoming more widely available in the 1970s and 1980s. Before then, computers were huge and expensive. Only large companies and institutions such as universities had computers.

But improved **technology** was allowing computers to be smaller and less expensive. More and more people were buying computers and learning how they worked. But some of these programmers started to use their skills to get into other computers for their own benefit.

Some of the earliest systems to be hacked were telephone systems. At the time, telephone calls were routed based on specific sounds, or tones. Some people started copying tones for long-distance routing so they could make free calls. These hackers became known as "phone phreaks."

One of the most famous phone phreaks was computer programmer John Draper. He built a device called a blue box.

John Draper based his blue box on the sound made by a toy whistle included in Cap'n Crunch cereal. Because of this, Draper became known as "Captain Crunch."

In 2017, hackers broke into the computer system of consumer credit reporting agency Equifax. More than 145 million accounts were affected. The hackers stole Social Security numbers, birth dates, addresses, credit card information, and more.

It could make the correct tones for hacking AT&T's phone lines. Draper was arrested for hacking for the first time in 1972. He was arrested several more times in the 1970s.

During the 1980s, there was a growing community of skilled hackers. They viewed themselves as **innovators**. Magazines, such as *Phrack* and *2600: The Hacker Quarterly*, were aimed at hackers. Secret hacker clubs began to form.

One of the most famous clubs was the Legion of Doom (LOD). It was started in 1984 by a hacker who called himself Lex Luthor. The group published journals for its members explaining how to hack systems. LOD members frequently hacked into systems, especially telecommunications systems. This was mostly to practice their skills and show other hackers what they could do. They generally didn't harm the systems they hacked into. In fact, some members were kicked out of LOD for causing harm.

In the 1980s and 1990s, laws were passed to stop hackers from misusing their abilities. In May 1990, the US **Secret Service** launched Operation Sundial. It was a plan to try and catch hackers. But hackers can be extremely difficult to track down. They can get in and out of computer systems without leaving a trace. Operation Sundial turned out to be a failure. Very few hackers were arrested.

By the 2000s, most people thought of hackers as criminals. Hackers started being regularly featured in the news. It seemed no one was safe from attack, not even the largest companies or law enforcement agencies. One of the biggest attacks in history happened to web service provider Yahoo in August 2013. More than 3 billion user accounts were hacked.

CHAPTER 6

HACKER ATTACK

Over the past decade, computer hacking has become big business. Since the mid-2000s, internet **scams** and computer viruses have become common. Black hat hackers sell their skills to criminals and others who want to harm people.

One method black hat hackers use is called phishing. This is a type of scam. The victims receive an email or text from a hacker. The hacker pretends to be someone the victim trusts, such as an **online** store or a friend. The hacker claims to need personal details, such as passwords or banking information. The hacker uses the information for personal gain. Common crimes include stealing from bank accounts and identity theft.

Malware is another way hackers harm people and damage computers. *Malware* is short for ***malicious software***. A virus is a type of malware. A virus is a program that changes the way a computer works. It can quickly spread from one computer to another. It may erase data and software.

Since 1991, Norton has been one of the most popular brands of antivirus and computer security software.

In the late 1980s, Steven Bellovin developed one of the first computer firewalls. He and William Cheswick created it while working at Bell Laboratories.

Other types of malware include Trojans, spyware, and ransomware. A Trojan looks like a program that is safe to use. However, it creates weaknesses in systems so that hackers can get in. Spyware learns victims' passwords, banking details, and more. Ransomware shuts down victims' computer systems until a **ransom** is paid.

Black hat hackers send malware through text and email attachments. When opened or clicked on, the malware begins to spread throughout the device. In 2017, 360,000 malware files were detected every day. White hat hackers work to find ways to stop malware from spreading.

There are several main methods for preventing hacks. One defense is a firewall. This is a system that keeps unwanted people from connecting to a computer **network**. Firewalls have to be updated often as hackers can eventually find their way around them.

Another defense is anti-malware **software**. This type of software scans devices for threats. The software can also prevent malware from getting into devices. And it removes any malware that it finds in the system.

Firewalls and anti-malware software are often used together to protect computer systems. But they are just two ways people can protect themselves from black hat hackers. New defenses are being developed all the time.

CHAPTER 7
HACKER REVOLUTION

New forms of hacking are forming all the time. One trend that started in the mid-1990s is hacktivism. The term *hacktivism* is a combination of *hack* and **activism**.

Hackers use hacktivism to promote causes that are important to them. They might write a message about the cause on a website that opposes the cause. They may **disrupt** traffic from visiting a site or redirect it to another site. This type of hacking usually doesn't harm the system being hacked. However, even if the hackers don't cause harm, it is usually still illegal.

Not all hacktivists are disruptive. **Random** Hacks of Kindness (RHoK) is a hacktivist group. It looks for **innovative** ways to use **technology** to solve problems around the world. RHoK holds events called hackathons. The group's goal is to use computers and other technologies to help people.

Organizations such as colleges and universities also use hackathons to spark innovation. Students from universities

RANDOM HACKS OF KINDNESS

RHoK was formed in 2009 by Microsoft, Google, Yahoo, **NASA**, and the World Bank. They wanted to focus on improving **disaster** relief efforts. Their idea was to combine the knowledge of disaster relief experts and programmers at hackathons held around the world.

During RHoK hackathons, the disaster relief experts give the hackers a problem to solve. Then they work on the problem for a couple of days and propose solutions. The disaster experts choose winning solutions to try in real disaster response situations.

The first hackathon took place at Hacker Dojo in Mountain View, California, in November 2009. Some of the **software** built at the event was used in relief efforts after the Haiti and Chile earthquakes in 2010. Since then, RHoK hackathons have been held every six months.

HACKER DOJO

Social media company Facebook often holds hackathons to come up with new features. Founder and CEO Mark Zuckerberg reviews the best ideas from each hackathon.

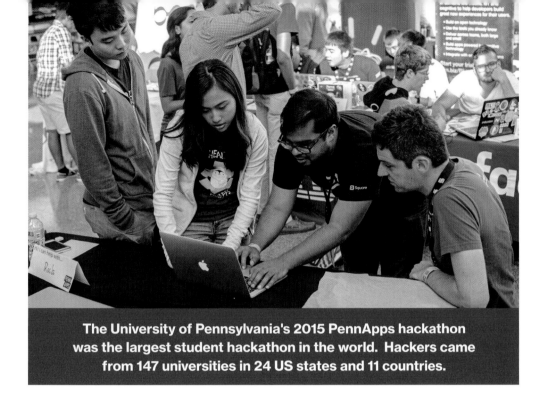

The University of Pennsylvania's 2015 PennApps hackathon was the largest student hackathon in the world. Hackers came from 147 universities in 24 US states and 11 countries.

around the world gather at events such as PennApps and MHacks. They learn how to use different kinds of **software** and computers, write new **code**, and come up with creative ideas.

These forms of hacking are more like what the original hackers of the 1960s did. Each day, hackers think of new ideas for computers and software. Good or bad, hackers are always pushing the limits to do things that have not been done before. No one knows what will come next. But hackers will definitely play a big part in the future of computers and **technology**.

TIMELINE

1970s
Computers start becoming more widely available.

1972
John Draper is arrested for hacking for the first time.

1960s
The word *hack* starts being associated with computer programming.

1984
The hacker club Legion of Doom (LOD) is formed.

1990
The federal government launches Operation Sundial to investigate hacking.

2009

Microsoft, Google, Yahoo, NASA, and the World Bank form RHoK. The first RHoK hackathon is held.

2013

More than 3 billion Yahoo accounts are hacked.

2017

360,000 malware files are detected every day.

2010

Software developed at a RHoK hackathon is used to help relief efforts after earthquakes in Haiti and Chile.

GLOSSARY

activism–a practice that emphasizes direct action in support of or in opposition to an issue that causes disagreement.

available–able to be had or used.

certification–official recognition that someone has fulfilled certain requirements.

code–a set of instructions for a computer.

cybercriminal–someone who commits a crime related to or using computers.

cybersecurity–measures taken to protect a computer or computer system against attack.

disaster–an event that causes damage, destruction, and often loss of life. Natural disasters include events such as hurricanes, tornadoes, and earthquakes.

disrupt–to throw into disorder.

ethical–morally right. Something unethical is morally wrong.

innovate–to come up with a new idea, method, or device. Something marked by a new idea, method, or device is innovative. Someone who innovates is an innovator.

malicious–having or showing a desire to cause harm to another person.

NASA–National Aeronautics and Space Administration. NASA is a US government agency that manages the nation's space program and conducts flight research.

network–a system of computers connected by communications lines.

online–connected to the internet.

random–lacking a definite plan or pattern.

ransom–money demanded for the release of a captured person or return of property.

scam–a fake or illegal act or operation.

Secret Service–a federal law enforcement agency. Its duties include conducting criminal investigations and protecting national leaders. This includes the president and visiting foreign leaders.

software–the written programs used to operate a computer.

technology (tehk-NAH-luh-jee)–machinery and equipment developed for practical purposes using scientific principles and engineering.

INDEX